# In The Bleak Midwinter

## A Christmas Carol

# Ken Pyne

THE KINGSWOOD PRESS

The Kingswood Press
an imprint of William Heinemann Ltd
10 Upper Grosvenor Street, London W1X 9PA

LONDON MELBOURNE
JOHANNESBURG AUCKLAND

First Published 1987

0 434 98124 9

Printed and bound in Great Britain by
Redwood Burn Ltd, Trowbridge, Wiltshire

*To*
*Santa*

# Christmas Eve

# Christmas Day

# Boxing Day

ONLY THREE HUNDRED AND SIXTY FIVE DAYS TO CHRISTMAS! AAAAAAAAAAHHH!